D1082175

PREFACE TO SPECIAL EDITION

October 26—November 2, 1969 is an important week. It marks
the merger of the separate Youth Weeks sponsored by the Department
of Youth Ministry, National Council of Churches and the National
CYO Federation, the Division of Youth Activities, U.S. Catholic
Conference.

During this week youth of all churches will join in prayer and study
as a preparation for a series of Community Service Projects relating
to this year's Youth Week theme: "White Plight? Racism in American
Society."

Hopefully this resource book will help us understand our prejudice
and encourage our efforts in working for solidarity in our churches
and communities. We feel it illustrates the roles youth have in the
crucial issue of racism. We commend it to your careful reflection and
study.

Thomas J. Leonard
Division of Youth Activities
U.S. Catholic Conference

Robert L. Pierce
Department of Youth Ministry
National Council of Churches

AM I A RACIST?

Compiled and edited by ROBERT HEYER
Photographs by FORTUNE MONTE
Designed by MARION FALLER
Coordinated by DONALD BROPHY

NATIONAL CYO FEDERATION
Division of Youth Activities
U.S. Catholic Conference

and

DEPARTMENT OF YOUTH
ACTIVITIES
National Council of Churches

Published by Paulist Press, editorial office 304 W. 58th Street, New York, N.Y., business office Glen Rock, N.J., and by Association Press, 291 Broadway, New York, N.Y.

Manufactured in the United States of America.

ACKNOWLEDGMENTS

HARPER & ROW
49 E. 33rd Street
New York, N.Y.

PSYCHOLOGY TODAY
© Communications/Research/Machines/Inc.
Del Mar, Calif.

CATHOLIC WORLD
304 W. 58th Street
New York, N.Y.

THE LIGUORIAN
Liguorian, Mich.

NEWSWEEK
444 Madison Avenue
New York, N.Y.

INTRODUCTION

"This is our basic conclusion: Our nation is moving toward two societies, one black, one white—separate and unequal . . . What white Americans have never fully understood—but what the Negro can never forget—is that white society is deeply implicated in the ghetto. White institutions created it, white institutions maintain it, and white society condones it."

Commission on Civil Disorders

"That's my opinion and it's very true" comes to our lips more easily than "I'm prejudiced." The Kerner Report on civil disorders, however, warns that our opinions are often biased. They are not based on facts but grow out of fear and ignorance. It warns that walls are being built in our cities, anger and hostility are spreading, attitudes are hardening. In fact what we Americans are rapidly constructing between white and black America will make the barbed wire Berlin wall look weak and insignificant. Our insensitivity to prejudice deepens; myths about housing values, neighborhood schools, and welfare increase destructive emotional responses to critical problems; political leaders continue to play on people's fears and ignore well-researched evidence of race problems.

This book is a modest attempt to confront personal and communal prejudice in order to break the wall of racism and dilute the deadly poison that threatens to split America into "two societies, one black, one white."

Selections from Martin Luther King, Jr. stress that we must search out now the real dimensions of peace and justice, that we must decide our goal, chaos or community, so that law and order may establish justice and make us free. This essential task is presented through the dark prism of a variety of viewpoints. There is a section on the daily life in black America, focusing on job and housing problems. Then the effect of white institutions—education, welfare, police, Church— is briefly highlighted. The final section presents black reactions to our critical situation. And the concluding essay of a Chicago teenager, "The Slum Is Me," spells out the challenges we face in renewing law and order and justice.

Hopefully this book will contribute to destroying some prejudice. In addition to religion class—Sunday school, CCD, or daily class—these pictures and selections would be very productive for meaningful discussions on retreats, at parent-teacher meetings, in adult education, or just within a family discussion. Good subway reading. It could also be a fruitful basis for white and black group dialogues.

Read the feeling! Sensitively feel along with the pictures. Reflect upon the quotes, honestly, openly. Answer the questions. Try to act out the picture-situations: take on the feelings and attitudes of the persons and act out a brief dialogue of the picture-situation. Share your views in small group discussions—not defending your own position, but a dialogue where you listen, you question, you search, you share your opinions, your fears, your hopes. Evaluate your previous attitudes. Look up further data on particular problem areas. Such an experience can break down the walls of prejudice and chaos so that you can find law and order in your own life, so that you can create our community in justice and freedom.

. . . And every now and then I wonder what I want him to say.

Tell him not to mention that I have a Nobel Peace Prize—that isn't important.

Tell him not to mention that I have 300 or 400 other awards—that's not important. Tell him not to mention where I went to school.

I'd like to mention that day that Martin Luther King, Jr. tried to give his life serving others.

I'd like for somebody to say that day that Martin Luther King, Jr. tried to love somebody.

I want you to say that I tried to be right and walk with them. I want you to be able to say that day that I did try to feed the hungry. I want you to say on that day that I did try in my life to clothe the naked. I want you to say on that day that I did try in my life to visit those in prison. And I want you to say that I tried to love and serve humanity.

Yes, if you want, say that I was a drum major. Say that I was a drum major for justice. Say that I was a drum major for peace, say that I was a drum major for righteousness.

Martin Luther King, Jr.

A TRIBUTE TO
MARTIN LUTHER KING Jr.
COMMEMORATIVE FLICKER PICTURE RINGS

IN MEMORY OF A GREAT AMERICAN

5¢

COMBAT!

TRADE THEM! COLLECT THEM! WEAR THEM!

folz VEND·O·MART

CHAIN LINKS

BE A FLOWER CHILD

1¢

HEY KIDS!
IT'S GREAT!

GOLD
BUBBLE GUM

POTATO CHIPS

T. SAIL
ECT KILLER

CHAOS OR COMMUNITY . . .

Half of all Negroes live in substandard housing, and Negroes have half the income of whites. When we turn to the negative experiences of life, the Negro has a double share. There are twice as many unemployed. The rate of infant mortality (widely accepted as an accurate index of general health) among Negroes is double that of whites. The equation pursues Negroes even into war. There were twice as many Negroes as whites in combat in Vietnam at the beginning of 1967, and twice as many Negro soldiers died in action (20.6 percent) in proportion to their numbers in the population.

In other spheres, the figures are equally alarming. In elementary schools, Negroes lag one to three years behind the whites, and their segregated schools receive substantially less money per student than do white schools. One twentieth as many Negroes as whites attend college, and half of these are in ill-equipped Southern institutions.

Of employed Negroes, 75 percent hold menial jobs. Depressed living standards for Negroes are not simply the consequence of neglect. Nor can they be explained by the myth of the Negroes' innate incapabilities, or by the more sophisticated rationalization of his acquired infirmities (family disorganization, poor education, etc.). They are a structural part of the economic system in the United States. Certain industries and enterprises are based upon a supply of low paid, underskilled and immobile nonwhite labor. Hard assembly factories, hospitals, service industries, housework, and agricultural operations using itinerant labor would suffer economic trauma, if not disaster, with a rise in wage scales.

Martin Luther King, Jr., WHERE DO WE GO FROM HERE: Chaos or Community, pp. 6–7.

TIME IS ALWAYS RIPE TO DO RIGHT . . .

. . . I had also hoped that the white moderate would reject the myth of time . . . It is a strangely irrational notion that there is something in the very flow of time that will inevitably cure all ills. Actually time is neutral. It can be used either destructively or constructively. I am coming to feel that the people of ill will have used time much more effectively than the people of good will. We will have to repent in this generation not merely for the vitriolic words and actions of the bad people, but for the appalling silence of the good people. We must come to see that human progress never rolls in on the wheels of inevitability. It comes from the tireless efforts and persistent work of men willing to be co-workers with God, and without this hard work time itself becomes an ally of the forces of social stagnation. We must use time creatively and forever realize that the time is always ripe to do right.

Martin Luther King, Jr., LETTER FROM BIRMINGHAM CITY JAIL.

11

MORALLY DISOBEYING THE LAW . . .

You express a good deal of anxiety over our willingness to break laws. This is certainly a legitimate concern. Since we so diligently urge people to obey the Supreme Court's decision of 1954 outlawing segregation in the public schools it is rather strange and paradoxical to find us consciously breaking laws. One may ask, "How can you advocate breaking some laws and obeying others?" The answer is found in the fact that there are two types of laws: there are just laws and there are unjust laws. I would be the first to advocate obeying just laws. Conversely, one has a moral responsibility to disobey unjust laws.

. . . Now what is the difference between the two? How does one determine when a law is just or unjust? A just law is a manmade code that squares with the moral law or the law of God. An unjust law is a code that is out of harmony with the moral law . . . I hope you can see the distinction I am trying to point out. In no sense do I advocate evading or defying the law as a rabid segregationist would do. This would lead to anarchy . . . I had hoped that the white moderate would understand that law and order exist for the purpose of establishing justice, and that when they fail to do this they become dangerously structured dams that block the flow of social progress.

Martin Luther King, Jr., LETTER FROM BIRMINGHAM CITY JAIL.

VIOLENCE VERSUS NONVIOLENCE . . .

To meet hate with retaliatory hate would do nothing but intensify the existence of evil in the universe. Hate begets hate, violence begets violence, toughness begets a greater toughness. We must meet the forces of hate with the power of love; we must meet physical force with soul force. Our aim must never be to defeat or humiliate the white man, but to aim to win his friendship and understanding.

Martin Luther King, Jr., STRIDE TOWARD FREEDOM, p. 87.

I have tried to stand between these two forces saying that we need not follow the "do-nothingism" of the complacent or the hatred and despair of the black nationalist. There is the more excellent way of love and nonviolent protest. I'm grateful to God that, through the Negro church, the dimension of nonviolence entered our struggle.

Martin Luther King, Jr., LETTER FROM BIRMINGHAM CITY JAIL.

The ultimate tragedy of Birmingham was not the brutality of the bad people, but the silence of the good people.

Martin Luther King, Jr., WHY WE CAN'T WAIT, p. 43.

Nonviolence is a powerful and just weapon. It is a weapon unique in history, which cuts without wounding and ennobles the man who wields it. It is a sword that heals. Both a practical and moral answer to the Negro's cry for justice, nonviolent direct action proved that it could win victories without losing wars, and so became the triumphant tactic of the Negro Revolution in 1963.

Martin Luther King, Jr., WHY WE CAN'T WAIT, p. 14.

Make no mistake, the American people are in part responsible for Martin Luther King's death. The assassin heard enough condemnation of King and of Negroes to know that he had public support. He knew that there were millions of people in the United States who wished that King were dead. He had support.

Dr. Benjamin Mays in his eulogy to Martin Luther King, Jr.

THE DREAM OF FREEDOM . . .

So even though we face the difficulties of today and tomorrow I still
have a dream. I have a dream that one day this nation will rise up and
live out the true meaning of its creed . . . that all men are created
equal. I have a dream that one day even the State of Mississippi, a
state sweltering with the heat of oppression, will be transformed into
an oasis of freedom and justice. I have a dream that one day my four
little children will live in a nation where they will not be judged by the
color of their skin but by the content of their character. I have a dream
today—and if America is to become a great nation, this must come
true.

So let freedom ring. From the prodigious hilltops of New Hampshire,
let freedom ring. From the mighty mountains of New York, let freedom
ring. From the heighening Alleghenies of Pennsylvania let freedom
ring. But not only that: Let freedom ring from Stone Mountain of
Georgia. Let freedom ring from every hill and molehill of Mississippi.
And when this happens, when we let it ring, we will speed that day
when all of God's children, black men and white men, Jews and
gentiles, Protestants and Catholics, will be able to join hands and sing
in the words of the old Negro Spiritual:

> Free at last, free at last,
> Thank God Almighty, we're free at last.

Martin Luther King, Jr.

Where is the light of the resurrection on the faces of the living?

DEATH AND RESURRECTION: HOPE AND FREEDOM

And those of you who believe in what Martin Luther King, Jr. stood for I would challenge you today to see that his spirit never dies and that we go forward from this experience, which to me represents the Crucifixion, on toward the resurrection and the redemption of the spirit.

How many times have I heard him say that with every Good Friday there comes Easter. When Good Friday came these are the moments in life when we feel that all is lost, and there is no hope. But then Easter comes as a time of resurrection, of rebirth, of hope and fulfillment. . . .

We are concerned about not only the Negro poor, but the poor all over America and all over the world. Every man deserves a right to a job or an income so that he can pursue liberty, life and happiness. Our great nation, as he often said, has the resources, but his question was: Do we have the will? Somehow I hope in this resurrection experience the will will be created within the hearts, and minds, and the souls, and the spirits of those who have the power to make these changes come about.

If this can be done, then I know that his death will be the redemptive force that he so often talked about. . . .

Mrs. Martin Luther King at Memphis City Hall.

A CONVERSATION . . .

MARY HARRINGTON HALL: At least ten Negroes were killed in Chicago riots after Martin Luther King's assassination. Mayor Daley's order that police should shoot to maim looters in Chicago and shoot to kill arsonists is really inciting to riot. It also shows a lot of confidence in police marksmanship.

KENNETH B. CLARK: His statement invites police to assume the role of judge and executioner rather than of law enforcer. And you are right. That statement invites riots. The prisoners of the ghetto are incited to engage in a game with police to see who shoots more accurately. And in that kind of a game there can be only one score—the ghetto resident can't win.

HALL: Neither can the police.

CLARK: Neither can Mayor Daley. America can't really contain the lawlessness of the ghetto as long as the pathology and inequities exist . . . What American people have to learn is that they really can't control or destroy Negroes without destroying themselves . . . America cannot commit genocide without at the same time committing suicide.

PSYCHOLOGY TODAY, June 1968, pp. 20–21.

What terrible fear or hatred would cause us to shoot looters? Prevent looting wherever possible. Stop looting where adequate force arrives too late to prevent it. Arrest looters, absolutely. But shoot looters and all human nature rebels at our excess.

Attorney General Ramsey Clark.

Was Mayor Daley's statement violent? If so, how? Why?

Is "genocide" an exaggerated opinion?

Do you agree with Ramsey Clark's view? Why?

"What terrible fear or hatred would cause us to shoot looters?"

How does one express and grow in "reverence for life"?

REFLECTIONS OF A NEGRO PRIEST . . .

When Americans board trains, planes, or busses, they seem to
scout the vehicle automatically for a double seat that is empty.
In case there are only single seats vacant, the tendency of
the travelers is to take a seat beside a member of their own
ethnic group, white next to white, Negro with Negro. They sit down
with such smug security that I have often wondered, "How does
one know that he is safe sitting with a member of his own
racial group?" The person chosen with such assurance could be
a pickpocket, a pimp, a psychopath or a murderer; and the one
we shun could be a saint. Yet we feel safe with no other grounds
than skin color. The race consciousness of our nation has given
a sense of insecurity and a feeling of danger to contact
with other groups.

Bernardin J. Patterson, O.S.B., CATHOLIC WORLD, Feb. 1965.

Do you agree that people act in this manner? Why?

What are the sources of your feelings?

How do you react?

FIRM CATHOLIC BELIEVER

I have just read "Black and White" in the May *Liguorian*.
Why bring back the Civil War? The Negroes have all the advantages
of the whites. What do they want? I'll tell you what they want—
they want to sleep and eat and marry the whites, that's what.
Then what kind of a race will this nation have? Nothing to be
proud of, I'll assure you. Their brains aren't the same as the whites,
their morals are lower due to this fact. Their mentality is low.
The only intelligent ones are the ones that have been mixed
by the low white trash.

They have fine brick schools and fine homes, entertainment.
They drive better and bigger cars than the average whites.
They have their country to go back to—Nigeria.

We have foreigners who come to this country. They establish cities
of their own and stick together. Let the Negroes do the same thing.
They aren't slaves anymore and they aren't treated as such.
Communism is probably the cause of this big problem.

I am a firm Catholic believer and I don't hate the Negro
or dislike them, but I don't think the Church should push this
Negro issue so hard. Let them be and why not leave the South
alone? All of these riots and speeches on civil rights have just caused
bitterness and tension between these two races.

Anonymous letter to the editor, LIGUORIAN, July 1968.

*What attitudes of this "firm Catholic believer" do you agree with?
Why?*

What do you disagree with? Why?

Act out this scene—the worker and the Man.

How do they feel?

How are they reacting?

Speak their conversation.

RICHER RICHER, POORER POORER . . .

. . . In the past two years the agricultural subsidies for cotton
production have been 1.8 billion dollars, which means that
"the basically rich cotton farmers . . . got in two years a subsidy
equal to one year of the poverty program." This subsidy was used
"to finance mechanization, to withdraw land from production,
and to force people off the land and into the cities."
Most of the immigrants into the cities have been Negroes;
all of them have been poor.

Michael Harrington in a speech quoted in the
WALL STREET JOURNAL, March 4, 1966.

"It is a delusion to presume that the self interest of middle class
Americans links them with the poor in the cities," Mayor Hugh
Addonizio of riot-blooded Newark told the President's Riot
Commission. "For rising expectations are not only a part of ghetto
life, but a part of American life. Affluent Americans are gripped
more by the need to buy a vacation home, a sports car for their
college bound son and a second color television set than they are
with sharing their affluence with the poor." But more sharing
there will have to be.

NEWSWEEK, Nov. 20, 1967.

Does self-interest link the middle class to the poor?

Why or why not?

ATTITUDES CONCERNING RELIEF . . .

Joseph A. Califano, Jr., a presidential assistant, said that of 7.3 million citizens receiving aid in 1966 under relief programs with federal support, only 50,000 (less than one percent) were able-bodied males "who may be capable of getting off relief through job placement or vocational training." He said the 1966 relief rolls included 3.5 million children "whose parents couldn't support them." The parents included 150,000 fathers—100,000 of whom were incapacitated—and 900,000 mothers.

Among the 8,250,000 Americans receiving some form of public aid in February 1967, 7,558,000 were under one of four programs:

    4,817,000 dependent children
      592,000 disabled persons
       83,000 needy blind
    2,066,000 needy aged

Also, 692,000 persons (alcoholics, misfits, etc.) were on "general assistance" supported by local tax funds.

Gary Lednar, unpublished article.

What is your attitude toward persons on relief? What is its source?

What proportion of those receiving aid do you base your attitude on?

How does one change his or others' attitudes?

Act out this scene.

What is each person—the man, the woman in white, teenage girls, fellows with signs—thinking, feeling?

Each play a part and talk out how he feels in this situation.

LAW AND RIOTS . . .

Appeals to reason are understandable; they reflect the sense of
responsibility of governmental and civil rights leaders. But they
certainly do not take into account the fact that one cannot expect
individuals who have been systematically excluded from the privileges
of the middle class life to view themselves as middle class or to
behave in terms of middle class values. Those who despair
in the ghetto, follow their own laws—generally the laws of unreason.
And though these laws in themselves are not moral, they have
moral consequences and moral causes.

The inmates of the ghetto have no realistic stake in respecting
property because in a basic sense they do not possess it.
They are possessed by it. Property is, rather, an instrument for
perpetuation of their own exploitation. Stores in the ghetto—
which they rarely own—overcharge for inferior goods.
They may obtain the symbols of America's vaunted high standard
of living—radios, TV's, washing machines, refrigerators, but usually
only through usurious carrying costs, one more symbol of the pattern
of material exploitation. They do not respect property because
property is almost invariably used to degrade them.

When Senator Robert Kennedy incisively observed, after Watts,
"There is no point in telling Negroes to observe the law . . .
It has almost always been used against them," it was described
by an individual who took the trouble to write a letter to
The New York Times as an irresponsible incitement to violence.
The bedeviling fact remains, however, that as long as institutionalized
forms of American racism persist, violent eruptions will continue
to occur in the Negro ghettoes. As Senator Kennedy warned:
"All those places—Harlem, Watts, South Side—
are riots waiting to happen."

Kenneth B. Clark, THE NEW YORK TIMES MAGAZINE, Sept. 5, 1965.

WHY RIOT? . . .

Few want to admit that for the bulk of Americans blackness is
synonymous with inferiority.
> "It is a restless new type of proletariat—
> and it revolts against the city itself."

This feeling clouds even the white perception of what the riots are
all about. Enlightened opinion—shared by men conducting the
presidential investigation of the disorders—is that the riots are
essentially a protest against the conditions of Negro life,
the denial of dignity, unemployment, bad housing, bad city services.
Still, surveys show that most whites are neither able to absorb
nor to accept that judgment. The prevalent white opinion
is that outside agitators and subversive troublemakers are to blame.

NEWSWEEK, Nov. 20, 1967.

Is blackness synonymous with inferiority? Why or why not?

*What do you think of the findings of the presidential investigation
of the civil disorders?*

WHY LOOT? . . .

Desire, need and an eagerness to "get back at whitey"
were the primary reasons expressed by those who acknowledged
they had looted clothing, food, liquor, and appliance stores here.

One young antipoverty worker who was pummeled by other youths
when he tried to convince them they should not risk death
"for a damn cheap suit in a credit house along 125th St."
said later:

"What whitey don't understand is that America is a damn rich
country, and she flashes this richness in the brother's face
and tells him 'it ain't for you.' "

THE NEW YORK TIMES, Apr. 9, 1968.

*Do you understand and/or sympathize with this need and
eagerness to "get back at whitey"?*

In the same situation what would you do?

COMMON HUMAN PREDICAMENT . . .

I remember coming home from school, you can guess how young
I must have been, and my mother asked me if my teacher
was colored or white, and I said she was a little bit colored
and a little bit white. . . . And as a matter of fact I was right.
That's part of the dilemma of being an American Negro;
that one is a little bit colored and a little bit white,
and not only in physical terms but in the head and in the heart.

James Baldwin, from THE NEGRO PROTEST, pp. 5–6.

The great tragedy but possibly the great salvation too
of the Negro and white in America is that neither one
can be free of the other. Each Negro is a little bit white
and each white is a little bit Negro, in the sense that neither
is totally alien from the other. Both are caught in a common
human predicament. Each one needs the other—the white to be free
from his guilt and the Negro to be free from his fear;
guilt and fear are both self destructive.

Kenneth B. Clark, THE DARK GHETTO, p. 223.

*Do you believe that each Negro is a little bit white and each
white is a little bit Negro?*

BREAKING THE GHETTO: HOPE . . .

Every time a Negro sees a group of secretaries—white and Negro—
chatting over lunch or children—white and Negro—walking to school
together, he feels that hope is possible. Every time his white friend
shows he is not afraid to argue with him as with anyone else,
he sees that freedom is possible, that there are some for whom
race is irrelevant, who accept or reject a person not as a Negro
or a white, but in terms of himself. Only so can the real confinements
of the ghetto be broken.

The Negro alone cannot win this fight that transcends
the "civil rights struggle." White and Negro must fight together
for the rights of human beings to make mistakes and to aspire
to human goals. Negroes will not break out of the barriers
of the ghettos unless whites transcend the barriers
of their own minds, for the ghetto is to the Negro
a reflection of the ghetto in which the white lives imprisoned.

Kenneth B. Clark, THE DARK GHETTO, p. 240.

Do you think that there is hope for integration?

*If so, how is this to be attained? How can you personnally
contribute to this goal?*

*If there is no hope for integration, what is the answer to our
racial strife? What would your personal response be in this
situation?*

41

BLACK AND WHITE AGONY . . .

This is our basic conclusion: Our nation is moving toward
two societies, one black, one white—separate and unequal.
Reaction to last summer's disorders has quickened the movement
and deepened the division. Discrimination and segregation have
long permeated much of American life; they now threaten
the future of every American.

The deepening radical division is not inevitable. The movement
apart can be reversed. Choice is still possible. Our principal task
is to define that choice and to press for a national resolution.

To pursue our present course will involve the continuing polarization
of the American community, and ultimately the destruction of basic
democratic values.

The alternative is not blind repression or capitulation to lawlessness.
It is the realization of common opportunities for all within
a single society.

The alternative will require a commitment to national action—
oompassionate, massive, and sustained, backed by the resources
of the most powerful and richest nation on this earth. From
every American it will require new attitudes, new understanding,
and, above all, new will.

REPORT OF THE NATIONAL ADVISORY COMMISSION ON CIVIL
DISORDERS (Henceforth referred to as the Commission on Civil Disorders).

Do you think the race crisis is really this serious?

How can the continuing polarization of the American community
destroy basic democratic values?

What are some dimensions of the new attitudes, new
understanding, and new will required as an alternative for
national action?

MYTH: The government has been building masses of new low-income houses for the poor in the cities, which the middle class has paid for and the poor have ruined.

FACT: In 30 years the Government has produced 600,000 new low-income dwelling units. In the same period, the Government tore down 700,000 low-income dwelling units to make way for urban renewal and new highways. But in that same period, the Government guaranteed $80 billion to subsidize 10 million moderate and medium-cost houses for whites in the suburbs, mostly through FHA, which up to last year had rules that effectively excluded Negroes. Many of these middle-class recipients of government subsidy are now saying, "We made it. Why can't they?"

Ben H. Bogdikian, THE SATURDAY EVENING POST, Aug. 10, 1968.

Was your viewpoint on low-income housing based more on myth or facts? Why?

If a great number of the people have strong attitudes based on myth, what are the consequences?

How would you help someone to change his attitude from myth-centered to a view more based on the real facts of this situation?

NATIVE RESERVES . . .

His housing is old, crumbling and rat-ridden, so desperately overcrowded that—at the density rates of parts of Harlem— the entire U.S. population could be squeezed into three of New York City's five boroughs. Garbage festers uncollected on the sidewalks; building codes go unenforced; the streets are not even paved in parts of Houston's black quarter. "The ghettos in America are like the native reserves in South Africa," says Ralph Bunche. "They symbolize the Negro as unacceptable, inferior and therefore kept apart."

NEWSWEEK, Nov. 20, 1967.

How much does this situation really concern the non-ghetto Americans?

Should they be seriously concerned? Why?

Concretely, how do you help others to become aware and involved?

. . . Nearly six million substandard housing units remain occupied in the United States. The housing problem is particularly acute in minority ghettos . . . many ghetto residents simply cannot pay the rent necessary to support decent housing. In Detroit, for example, over 40% of the non-white occupied units require rent of over 35½% of the tenant's income.

COMMISSION ON CIVIL DISORDERS.

Is 35½% of income for rent a very large figure?

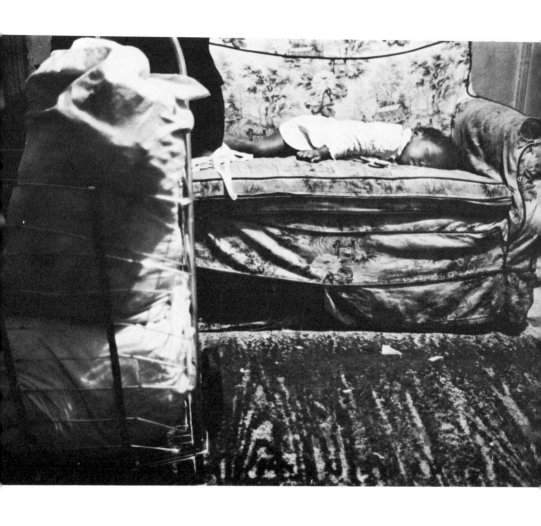

THE GHETTO THAT BLEW UP . . .

Forty years ago in Shaw Negroes and whites of moderate means
and like background lived side by side in homes that most owned.
But in the 1930's during the mass migration of Negroes
from the deep South whites began to flee. Many sold their homes
but often kept ownership of the stores. Slumlords milked the rents
and did little to maintain buildings, while city services slowed
to a trickle. By 1960, the year that the District of Columbia
took on a Negro majority, Shaw was 90% non-white,
50% deteriorated, and largely absentee owned, the money that
Shaw people paid to landlords and merchants rarely staying
in the community. Today, a third of Shaw's families live on
$3,000 a year or less. They pay half their income for rent
and must move often when they cannot find the $75 to $150 needed
each month to pay for dilapidated, rat-terrorized quarters.
Babies in Shaw are three times more likely to die
than in the rest of the city; the community requires five times more
welfare services than Washington as a whole. One typical welfare
mother told me that she rarely can afford enough food
for her children's breakfasts and sometimes keeps them home
from school rather than have them go there hungry and return
to hunger too. Meat and chicken are only possible early in the month,
right after the welfare check comes. The last two weeks,
fried potatoes and onions are the daily diet.

Dorothy Gilliam, McCALL'S, July, 1968.

How would you feel if you grew up in Shaw?

What effects would living daily with fear of rat-bite have on you?

Who is to blame for the ghetto?

How can we cure this disease?

LAW AND ORDER . . .

In 1966, the Commission's New Jersey State Advisory Committee was told that 16 years after passage of the New Jersey law prohibiting discrimination in housing, four of Newark's 13 public housing developments were 90 to 99 percent Negro. Of three housing developments for the elderly opened in Newark in 1965, one was 97 percent white and one was 92 percent Negro. Similarly, although racial designations have been removed from the public housing projects in Nashville, 12 of the 14 low-rent public housing projects there are more than 99 percent Negro or 99 percent white.

A TIME TO LISTEN . . . A TIME TO ACT: 1967 Report of the U.S. Commission on Civil Rights, p. 64. (Henceforth referred to as A TIME TO LISTEN).

What do you think are the most important laws in maintaining peace and order in a city?

What are your civil rights laws concerning integration of schools, integrated housing, and equal job opportunities?

Do discrimination practices of government agencies express public opinion or manipulate it?

SHARING BATHROOM . . .

Nearly 1.7 million Negro families, 29% of the total, live in substandard housing; 28% are overcrowded. In the cities, 15% of black families have no hot water, 15% share bathrooms with other families, and 21% have no bathtub or shower available.

NEWSWEEK, Nov. 20, 1967.

EXCLUDED FROM WHITE AREAS . . .

Thousands of Negro families have attained incomes, living standards, and cultural levels matching or surpassing those of whites who have "upgraded" themselves from distinctly ethnic neighborhoods. Yet most Negro families have remained in predominantly Negro neighborhoods, primarily because they have been effectively excluded from white residential areas.

COMMISSION ON CIVIL DISORDERS.

Does this attitude of exclusion nourish freedom and democratic values in the people—black and white?

If you were convinced, how would you go about sharing your conviction that integrated neighborhoods are good and beneficial?

INTEGRATION AND PROPERTY VALUES

Another authoritative study of the question merits attention: Luigi Laurenti's *Property Values and Race* (U. of California Press). It includes a five-year analysis of 10,000 home sales in Oakland, San Francisco, and Philadelphia, undertaken with the aid of expert appraisers and local brokers, and including data based on years of research. Contrary to the myth, this study shows that when neighborhoods were racially mixed, only 15% showed a drop in property values, while in 40% there was no difference, and in 45% property values rose appreciably.

AMERICA, March 11, 1967.

What do the studies show about the changes in property values when nonwhite families move into the neighborhood?

How do you feel about property values and racial integration? Why?

Do studies of this kind change basic attitudes and feelings? Why or why not?

LIVING IN CENTRAL HARLEM . . .

Central Harlem crowds 232,792 people within its three and one-half
square mile area. This represents over 100 people per acre . . .
About 10% of the area consists of parks and playgrounds,
compared to over 16% for New York City as a whole . . .
and much of this area is virtually useless because the parks are built
on extremely steep hills.

The 87,369 housing units in the area are divided among four
building types:

      1. "old law" tenements built between 1880 and 1901 (40%)
      2. "new law" tenements, 1901–1929 (15%)
      3. brownstones, 1901–1929 (35%)
      4. multi-dwelling buildings built since 1929 (10%)

It is clear that over 90% of the buildings in the area are over
38 years old, and nearly half were built before the turn
of the century.

YOUTH IN THE GHETTO, Harlem Youth Opportunities Unlimited.

THIRTY YEAR DEPRESSION . . .

In 1964, the nation's production has hit historic heights.
Yet U.S. government statistics reveal that the unemployment rate
of Negro youth averages 33 percent. In some of the northern ghettos
the rate of unemployment of youth is 50 percent. These figures
of unemployment dwarf even those of the depression of the 1930's,
and they shed some light on why there was such a high proportion
of young people in last summer's riots. Despair made them
active participants.

Charges that Negroes are going "too fast" are both cruel and
dangerous. The Negro is not going nearly fast enough, and claims
to the contrary only play into the hands of those who believe
that violence is the only means by which the Negro
will get anywhere.

Martin Luther King, Jr., SATURDAY EVENING POST, Nov. 7, 1964.

MEASURING THE JOB PROBLEM . . .

One measure of the job problem alone is the fact that the
unemployment rate among Negroes is 6.4 percent, twice that
of whites, and among young Negroes, who are often the most restless
and riot-prone, is a staggering 24.7 percent. Negroes also,
of course, need decent homes, better recreational facilities
for their children, help for their own struggling businesses.

NEWSWEEK, July 1, 1968.

A Labor Department study of ten of the nation's worst slums
found one Negro in three either jobless or earning too little
to live on—a statistic that makes even the official unemployment rate
of 9.3 percent for slum Negroes sound almost cheery.
And so the Negro underclass grows larger and more dangerous,
its probrems so stubbornly intractable to conventional cures that—
according to the labor study—no conceivable amount of economic
growth could "stir these backwaters."

NEWSWEEK, Nov. 20, 1967.

If he is working, a Negro is much more likely than a white man
to be in a menial and unpromising job. Negroes make up 11 percent
of the labor force but have only 6 percent of the nation's
professional and technical jobs, 3 percent of the managerial jobs,
6 percent of jobs in skilled trades. Their median family income
is only 58 percent of the white man's.

NEWSWEEK, Nov. 20, 1967.

UNDEREMPLOYED . . .

Pervasive unemployment and underemployment are the most persistent and serious grievances in minority areas. They are inextricably linked to the problem of civil disorder. . . . Despite growing Federal expenditures for manpower development and training programs, and sustained general economic prosperity and increasing demands for skilled workers, about two million— white and non-white—are permanently unemployed. About 10 million are underemployed, of whom six and a half million work full time for wages *below* the poverty line.

COMMISSION ON CIVIL DISORDERS.

Do you believe 6.5 million of the 10 million underemployed work full time for wages below the poverty line?

What do these job facts add up to in terms of the good order of the community?

What solutions did the Commission on Civil Disorders strongly suggest in this problem area?

Mrs. Willia Johnson, Supervisory Caseworker for the Lake County (Indiana) Department of Public Welfare, stated . . . that "many fathers desert their families rather than see them suffer from inability to provide their basic needs." Mrs. McCreary testified in Cleveland:

"This is how me and my husband got separated when he got out of his job and he went out to relief to get help and they refused to help . . . this is one reason we separated and divorced. He couldn't see his kids go hungry so he just left. He couldn't afford four, so he just left."

In Newark, a former caseworker for the Newark-Essex County Welfare Board stated that "the welfare system in this State forces the father out of the home and keeps the father out of the home."

A TIME TO LISTEN, p. 33.

What do you see in the eyes of these persons?

BLACK BETTERMENT IS SEPARATION . . .

The United States is a white man's country conducted according
to white customs and white laws for white purposes.
And it must be acknowledged that 89% of Americans are non-black.
I would not even make the argument that whites should not run
the country for their own interests. I would argue that whites
do not see, except in perilous self-defeat, that racial integration
is one of these interests. I believe that the white attitude towards
blacks is generally benign except when black claims intrude on
the majority's privileges or peace of mind. Whites have little objection
to bettering the condition of black lives as long as it does not cost
much and as long as it leads to the continuance of blacktowns
and so does not present the threat of genuine integration
at any level. The white condition for black betterment is,
to put it simply, separation.

W. H. Ferry, THE CENTER MAGAZINE, March 1968.

*Is racial integration in housing and jobs one of the white man's
self–interests?*

*Are you interested in integration? How do you express your
interest?*

INCOME GAP WIDENS . . .

According to the Commission Report "Negro family income is not keeping pace with white family income growth. In constant 1965 dollars, median non-white income in 1947 was $2147 lower than median white income. By 1966, the gap had grown to $3036." The country gets richer, but the Negro, although gaining a little, falls farther behind the whites. This hardly makes for a calm mind and a temperate, judicial consideration of the whys and wherefores and of the contemplated long-range improvements.

COMMISSION ON CIVIL DISORDERS.

Does this widening income gap foster disorder and violence?

But who would be responsible?

DESTROYING FAMILIES . . .

Many Negro men flee their families because they have lost their self-respect as husbands and fathers. The main reason for this is their inability to adequately support their families either because of unemployment or a lack of sufficient salary. The percentage of non-white families headed by a woman is 23.7 percent as compared to 8.9 percent among whites. As a result of the financial handicap on a fatherless home, many mothers must work to provide support for the family.

R. Heinemann, unpublished article.

UNIONS BLOCK JUSTICE . . .

Our labor unions, which have a history of fighting for justice
for the working man, are now blocking any serious economic justice
for the Negro and for other non-white minorities in our nation.

Kenneth B. Clark, PSYCHOLOGY TODAY, June 1968.

David F. Major, a Negro painting contractor, drew a similar picture
of the situation in Boston:

"In 1960, there were 1,297 apprentices in the building trades
in Massachusetts and only 15 were Negro. In 1965 there were 2,680
apprentices and still only 15 were Negroes. I know of many Negroes
who have tried to join unions but have been refused. . . .

"Because the construction labor force is smaller than needed here,
they have to fill vacancies with men imported from other States.
In all this the Negro is left out. The local unions are almost all-white
and the imported labor is all-white. So the Negro is either left
unemployed or underemployed . . ."

A TIME TO LISTEN, p. 53.

In 1966, the population of Cleveland was roughly 34 percent Negro. Plumbers Union Local 55 in Cleveland had four Negro members out of a total of 1,428 licensed journeymen. The first Negro members were admitted in 1964 after picketing of a federally assisted construction project by civil rights groups. There were no Negroes among the 1,786 journeymen ironworkers; and only one of the ironworkers' apprentices was Negro. There was a single Negro among the 1,519 journeymen pipefitters; all of the pipefitters' 80 apprentices were white.

In Oakland, where the population is about 36 percent nonwhite, and in San Francisco, where it is about 25 percent, it was not possible to obtain exact information on the number of minority workers in each craft union. Negro membership in Local 3, Operating Engineers, whose jurisdiction includes the Bay Area, has been estimated at 30 Negro members out of 9,000. Of the 3,000 members in the Plumbers Union Local 38, which also operates in the Bay Area, 20 were Negroes.

A TIME TO LISTEN, pp. 52–53.

Pointing to a recent report from the Department of Labor showing that the percentage of non-whites in apprentice trades rose from 1.69 percent in 1959 to 2.7 percent today, he snapped: "If this is progress, God help us. The Negro will never catch up."

NEWSWEEK, July 1, 1968.

Consult the union apprenticeship programs in the trades— plumbing, printing, building, carpentry, electrical, metal—and find out the racial makeup of the enrollees. Search out the reasons why there are so relatively few Negroes.

Do unions which practice a segregation policy indirectly promote violence?

BUSINESSMAN'S OPPORTUNITY . . .

But as Inland Steel's Bill Caples summed up for a lot of businessmen: "The real problem here is that people have to get their hands dirty. You can't sit in your living room . . . or your boardroom . . . and moan about 'the problem.' And you have to realize that in dealing with employment you're only dealing with half the problem. The thing you have to do in the community as a businessman is go beyond that . . . To work to improve housing, health, education. My own feeling is that business has belatedly come to the realization that we have a terrible problem and we must participate in its solution. We have to make the Negro equal—all equal. And, I'll make this statement," Bill Caples concluded, "that we either make an inroad on this problem . . . and make it now . . . or it carries with it the seeds of destruction of this society."

Leo Beebe, a dynamic, 50 year old Ford Vice President . . . is himself a new believer. "I used to sit in my office at Ford and receive memo after memo from Mr. Ford telling me I'd better hire some Negroes," he recalled. "I kept throwing the memos away. Mr. Ford was dedicated to that approach, but I wasn't. I looked at it this way: I said I refuse to hire any man for a job on any other criteria than his competence to do the job. And I was right.

"But," Beebe added, "I was stupid for the times. Hiring the most qualified man is a good philosophy—the right philosophy— so long as you give everybody the opportunity to be qualified. That simply has not been possible for many Negroes. I think it's just plain wrong not to correct that situation now." Nor was Beebe bashful about bracing businessmen. As he put it: "If I'm passing the plate, I can't tell whether a man's giving because he thinks it's right or because he's afraid or because he's intimidated by his neighbor. At the moment, I'm interested in the commitment—whatever the reason."

NEWSWEEK, July 1, 1968.

ARE WE INTERESTED . . . ?

Achieving that movement while there is still time is the heart
of the problem. Why can't history's most affluent, technologically
advanced society act to make the black man a full participant
in American life? The answer is a meld of ignorance, indifference,
bigotry, and callousness, escapism and sincere confusion.
But the inescapable truth is that so far America hasn't wanted to.
On that point there is indeed an American consensus—spelled out
rather clearly the way a democratic society allocates its resources.
America spends $75 billion for defense but only $7 billion on welfare
for the poor; $17.4 billion for tobacco and liquor but only $1.6
billion for the war on poverty; $3.2 billion for cosmetics and
toiletries but only $4 million a year for the training
of adult unemployed.

NEWSWEEK, Nov. 20, 1967.

FAREWELL TO INTEGRATION . . .

The vast fuss today about improvements in blacktown is not aimed
at integration. Few are afflicting us any longer with such a
troublesome lie. All these measures are primarily aimed at the
prevention of civic commotions, secondarily at assuaging the
conscience of whitetown, and finally at helping the blacks.
Priorities tell the story. In the last seven years we have spent
$384 billion on war, $27 billion on space, and less than $2 billion
on community development and housing.

W. H. Ferry, THE CENTER MAGAZINE, March, 1968.

78

FAILURE FACTORY . . .

The average slum is a failure factory. It should be closed.
It spends less money on the ghetto child than on other students,
gives him the least competent teachers with the largest teaching
loads, puts him in the most overcrowded schools and uses the most
unsuccessful curriculum. The longer the child stays in school,
the lower his achievement in reading and math, the lower his I.Q.

Ben H. Bagdikian, THE SATURDAY EVENING POST, Aug. 10, 1968.

DEMOCRATIC EDUCATION . . .

For many minorities, and particularly for the children of the ghetto,
the schools have failed to provide the educational experience
which could overcome the effects of discrimination and deprivation.
The bleak record of public education for ghetto children is growing
worse. In the critical skills—verbal and reading ability—
Negro students are falling further behind whites with each year
of school completed. The high unemployment and underemployment
rate for Negro youth is evidence, in part, of the growing educational
crisis . . . For example . . . twenty-five school boards in communities
surrounding Detroit spent up to $50 more per pupil per year
to educate their children than did the city.

COMMISSION ON CIVIL DISORDERS.

Compare "failure factory" with your own educational experience.

*What is the difference in the per pupil spending for inner city
and suburban school system in your area? Is there a significant
difference? Why?*

*"Negro students are falling further behind whites with each year
of school completed." Why? What would you do if your son was
in this situation?*

Who is responsible for the failure of the ghetto schools?

THE GHETTO SHOOL . . .

John Solar, Executive Director of the Harlem Neighborhood
Association and a resident of Harlem, told the New York Advisory
Committee: "Now it really isn't . . . necessary to say to a person,
'I am sorry; you can't have the job because you are a Negro.'
What happens more frequently now is that they say, 'You can't have
the job because you are not properly educated, you are not
motivated, you are not prepared.' This is quite damning because
you see how this prejudice has operated for so long that now
it's no longer necessary to say, 'I don't want you because you are
black. I don't want you because you are just not prepared'—
and it has been an educational system that has worked
to create this condition."

A TIME TO LISTEN, p. 41–42.

*What effect do you think private and parochial schools have on
segregation in the public school? Why?*

*If a parochial school or private school system contributed to de
facto segregation in public schools, how should the Christian
school or system best give witness to its duty of service? Why?*

HIDDEN CURRICULUM . . .

Dr. Charles Pinderhughes, a psychiatrist, explained in Boston
that children learn from each other by means of a "hidden
curriculum": "What the pupils are learning from one another
is probably just as important as what they are learning from
the teachers. This is what I refer to as the hidden curriculum.
It involves such things as how to think about themselves,
how to think about other people, and how to get along with them.
It involves such things as values . . . codes, and . . .
styles of behavior. . . ."

A TIME TO LISTEN, p. 45.

How are your values influenced by your peer group?

BLACK STUDENTS TELL IT LIKE IT IS . . .

The outspoken students insist that they will no longer be trained
as imitation white people for an inferior place in a racist society.
One of them—and it was difficult to judge how representative
he was—spoke of achieving full liberalization of the Negro now
or of destroying the society that keeps him in bondage.
Even allowing for youthful revolutionary rhetoric, the Howard students
made it perfectly clear that they are no longer prepared
to accept second best in American society.

THE NEW YORK TIMES, July 7, 1968.

*What does it mean for a Negro to become an "imitation white"
man?*

Is it revolutionary rhetoric or telling it like it is?

DESIGNED TO SAVE MONEY . . .

Our present system of public welfare is designed to save money
instead of people, and tragically ends up by doing neither.
This system has two critical deficiencies:

First, it excludes large numbers of persons who are in great need
and who, if provided a decent level of support, might be able
to become more productive and self-sufficient. No federal funds
are available for millions of men and women who are needy
but neither aged, handicapped, nor the parents of minor children.

Second, for those included, the system provides assistance well below
the minimum necessary for a decent level of existence, and imposes
restrictions that encourage continued dependency on welfare
and undermine self-respect.

COMMISSION ON CIVIL DISORDERS.

*Do you think the people now excluded, "if provided a decent
level of support, might be able to become more productive and
self-sufficient"?*

*What is the minimum level income necessary for a decent
existence for a family of four? What is the average yearly welfare
payment for such a family in your community?*

WELFARE ACCORDING TO LAW AND ORDER . . .

Since very few of those eligible actually participate in welfare
(varying from 25% to 50%), and since the people who do participate
rarely receive the full amount entitled to them, what would happen
if all the eligible claimed all their *rights*? It is quite possible, even
probable, that the system would break down and fall apart.

Gary Lednar, unpublished article.

*Do you think poor people should be helped to obtain all their
legal rights prescribed in welfare laws? If so, how?*

EASY SLUM LIVING . . .

Mrs. Jacqueline Taylor, appearing at an open meeting of the Indiana Advisory Committee in Gary, was asked to comment on the statement often made that "ADC mothers have it pretty easy." She replied:

"I have heard people say that lots of times. They think we have it so easy. I would like to see anyone, anyone, step forward, to change his good job for my position, his nice home—you know—just his nice position.

"In other words, if he wants my place, let him take it for a couple of months. Just a couple of months, that's all. Let him come forward, smell the garbage in the summertime, fight the rats, freeze in the wintertime . . . Let him take it; let him try to feed five children from 17 to 5 on $167 a month."

A TIME TO LISTEN, p. 30.

What is an "ADC mother"?

Do many express the attitude first noted? What are their reasons?

Some people say: "They're happy. They don't know any better. Don't disturb them." How do you feel?

EXPLOITING YOUR NEIGHBOR . . .

Similarly, Mrs. Fields told the Indiana State Advisory Committee that because welfare mothers in Gary cannot get credit from large chain stores to purchase such a necessary item as a gas heater, they generally have to patronize small furniture stores which "charge you twice what the thing costs."

A TIME TO LISTEN, p. 37.

Who are the exploiters? Who are exploited?

POLICE AND COMMUNITY . . .

The abrasive relationship between the police and the minority communities has been a major—and explosive—source of grievance, tension and disorder. The blame must be shared by the total society. The police are faced with demands for increased protection and service in the ghetto. Yet the aggressive patrol practices thought necessary to meet these demands themselves create tension and hostility. The resulting grievances have been further aggravated by the lack of effective mechanisms for handling complaints against the police.

COMMISSION ON CIVIL DISORDERS.

What do the police represent to you, to the people of the ghetto?

"The blame must be shared by the total society." Must it? Your reasons?

What is an aggressive patrol practice? Why are they thought necessary?

POLICE PROTECTION . . .

Christopher Hayes, Chairman of the Boston South End Federation of Citizens Organizations, stated: "Police have isolated the South End as an area, giving it only token protection. Prostitution, bookmaking and after-hour places are all over, and there is an excess of liquor stores and a shortage of foot patrolmen to keep the street safe. A hotel located near police headquarters, and known throughout the city as a house of prostitution, was closed by police after a Boston newspaper publicized it. But it opened again after about two months and is now back in business.

A TIME TO LISTEN, p. 22.

What determines how much police protection an area gets? How influential are citizens in the decision?

RACISM IN CHURCHES? . . .

Our churches make words; they pass resolutions. But there has been no evidence that the churches have found the strength, the courage, or the practical know-how to use religious institutions as instruments for bringing about the kind of maturity that our schools have not provided.

Kenneth B. Clark, PSYCHOLOGY TODAY, June, 1968.

What is the Church?

How does a religious institution change from do-nothingism to become an instrument of social change?

PASTOR PREACHES, PEOPLE LEAVE . . .

Rev. Londagin described how the church membership reacted to his activities in behalf of open housing: "When we took strong positions on certain issues, a large percentage of the church membership deserted the congregation."

He described the expressed concern of the people who left: "Well, the first response, by and large, was: 'Well, we like the Negroes; we have many Negro friends and are not really against equal rights, but the Church has no business talking about it from the pulpit, and we want to hear nothing but the gospel.' "

A TIME TO LISTEN, p. 79.

"We want to hear nothing but the gospel." What is the gospel?

"The Church has no business talking about it from the pulpit." Does it?

THE PREJUDICED CHRISTIAN . . .

Among white Protestant and Catholic church members in California, nearly half say they would move if several Negro families moved into their block. A third think Negroes less intelligent; and nearly half blame communists and other radicals for racial tensions. These data were collected in 1963 before any riots. Undoubtedly things are worse today.

THE NEW YORK TIMES, March 26, 1968.

Would you move if several Negro families moved into your block?

Are Negroes less intelligent?

Are communists and other radicals responsible for racial tensions?

RELIGION AND WHITE RACISM . . .

No one observing the history of the Church in America can deny the shameful fact that it has been an accomplice in structuring racism into the architecture of American society. A religion true to its mission knows that segregation is morally wrong and sinful. It is unbrotherly and impersonal. Two segregated souls can never meet God.

The Church must take the lead in social reform. It must move out into the arena of life . . . And it must lead men along the right path of true integration, something the law cannot do.

Martin Luther King, Jr., THE CRITIC, June-July, 1967.

How has the Church been racist?

Why can't the law "lead men along the path of true integration"?

THE NEWS MEDIA AND RACISM . . .

The Commission recommends that the media:

Expand coverage of the Negro community and of race problems through permanent assignment of reporters familiar with urban and racial affairs, and through establishment of more and better links with the Negro community.

Integrate Negroes and Negro activities into all aspects of coverage and content, including newspaper articles and television programming. The news media must publish newspapers and produce programs that recognize the existence and activities of Negroes as a group within the community and as a part of the larger community.

Recruit more Negroes into journalism and broadcasting and promote those who are qualified to positions of significant responsibility. Recruitment should begin in high schools and continue through college.

COMMISSION ON CIVIL DISORDERS.

How important is it to have reporters "familiar with urban and racial affairs"?

What are your feelings concerning each of the commission's suggestions?

BECOMING A DIVIDED NATION . . .

There was a remarkable unanimity on the part of the ghetto residents about their major grievances. The commission listed them in order of the intensity of feeling they aroused: 1. Police practices, 2. Unemployment and "underemployment" (part-time or unsteady jobs), 3. Poor housing, 4. Poor education, 5. Poor recreation facilities and programs, 6. Ineffective grievance mechanisms, 7. Disrespectful white attitudes, 8. Discriminatory justice, 9. Inadequate federal programs. 10. Poor municipal services, 11. Discriminatory commercial and credit practices, 12. Inadequate welfare programs.

The Negro population is growing "significantly faster" than the white population, and it is younger. The median age of American Negroes is 21.1, of whites 29.1. One out of nine Americans was black in 1966; by 1972 the proportion will be one out of eight. The great majority of Negroes (70%) live in cities to which they have migrated in the last fifty years from the rural South. The white population has steadily moved to the suburbs, which are 96% white.

Negroes with the same education and the same jobs as whites are paid less. For the same housing units, Negroes pay an average 10% higher rent.

More than 2.3 million Negro children under 15 are living in circumstances below the poverty level ($3,335 a year for a family of four).

Black mothers die in childbirth almost four times as often as white mothers do; black babies die in infancy almost three times as often as white babies. A Negro's life expectancy is 64.1 years, a white's 71 years.

Donald Jackson, LIFE, March 8, 1968.

If any man is rich,
but shuts his eyes
to one who stands in need,
the love of God
is missing from his heart.
"If any man is rich
and does give help
to one who stands in need,
he only gives the poor man
what was already his.
The earth was made for all,
not just for the rich."
So wrote St. Ambrose.
The Church has always taught
that not for any man
is private property
an absolute unbridled right.
The Church has always taught
that any conflict
between the rights of private property
and the basic rights of the community
must be resolved
by public authority,
that is, by government
with the help of all.

Pope Paul VI, POPULORUM PROGRESSO, trans. by R. V. Bogan in U.S.
CATHOLIC, Aug. 1968.

It is sometimes difficult to determine which are the deepest wounds,
the physical or the psychological. Only a Negro understands the
social leprosy that segregation inflicts upon him.

Martin Luther King, Jr., THE CRITIC, June-July 1967.

Is it true "all you need is love"?

THE STORM WHICH RAGES . . .

Please try to be clear, dear James, through the storm which rages about your youthful head today, about the reality which lies behind the words "acceptance" and "integration." There is no reason for you to try to become like white people, and there is no basis whatever for their impertinent assumption that *they* must accept *you*. The really terrible thing, old buddy, is that *you* must accept *them*. And I mean that very seriously. You must accept them and accept them with love. For these innocent people have no other hope. They are, in effect, still trapped in a history which they do not understand; and until they understand it, they cannot be released from it.

James Baldwin, THE FIRE NEXT TIME, p. 22.

Who are "they"? Are you one of them?

Are "they" innocent? Who must accept who?

A society that has done something special *Against* the Negro for hundreds of years must now do something special *For* him, in order to equip him to compete on a just and equal basis.

Martin Luther King, Jr., THE CRITIC, June-July, 1968.

Do you agree? If so, whose job is it to do things for *the Negro? Is it yours?*

Negro Sprinter Tommie Smith says: "On the track, you're Tommie Smith, the fastest man in the world, but off it you are just another nigger."

W. H. Ferry, THE CENTER MAGAZINE, March, 1968.

Do you think like this? Do you treat all Negroes in the same manner? Do you treat all whites in the same way?

As Malcolm X put it: "No sane black man really wants integration . . . No sane black man believes that the white man will ever give the black man anything more than token integration."

Do you think he is correct? Do you want more than token integration? Why? Or, why not?

What white Americans have never fully understood, but what the Negro can never forget, is that white society is deeply implicated in the ghetto. White institutions created it. White institutions maintain it, and white society condones it.

COMMISSION ON CIVIL DISORDERS.

What has been America's reaction to this indictment? Why?

BAYARD RUSTIN'S VIEWPOINT . . .

There can be only two responses to the commission's "white racism" charge. On the one hand, there are certain whites with a "guilt complex," masochists anxious to let the Negro know of their guilt— these are the kinds of whites that disgust me and offend other Negroes. On the other hand, there are more healthy people who, however, admit racism is so deep and profound a problem that they can simply opt out and do nothing.

Will "guilty" people genuinely be able to help the black community?

Do you feel that racism is so deep and profound a problem that you can do nothing?

IS LOVE REALLY NECESSARY? . . .

It would be unrealistic, of course, to expect the masses of whites and Negroes who have grown up in an essentially racist society suddenly to love one another. Fortunately love is not a prerequisite for the social reorganization now demanded. Love has not been necessary to create workable living arrangements among other ethnic groups in our society. It is no more relevant to ask Negroes and whites to love each other than to ask Italians and Irish to do the same as a prerequisite for social peace and justice.

Kenneth B. Clark, THE NEW YORK TIMES MAGAZINE, Sept. 5, 1965.

What is necessary to create workable living arrangements in black and white America?

POWERLESSNESS OF THE NEGRO COMMUNITY . . .

The Massachusetts State Advisory Committee, summarizing what it has heard at open meetings in March and April of 1966, reported: "A recurring theme during the four days of meetings was the powerlessness of the Negro community. Whether the people were discussing housing, employment, welfare, the poverty program, education, or municipal services, they inevitably made the point that no one listens to them, no one considers their needs. More than a score of speakers pointed out to the Committee that the Negro in Boston is devoid of political power."

A TIME TO LISTEN, p. 7.

How important is it to consult and listen to the Negro community? Why?

Is the Negro the only group that feels so powerless?

What does the feeling of powerlessness lead to?

WHITE MAN'S BENEVOLENCE

When the Reverend Albert Cleage turned down $100,000 from well-meaning Detroiters because there were white strings on the grant he provided millions of dollars worth of pride and self-confidence to blacktowns everywhere. It is possible to reject the white man's benevolence!

W. H. Ferry, SATURDAY REVIEW, June 15, 1968.

What would you have done? Why?

SEEING CLEARLY . . .

In Cleveland, Dr. Robert Coles, a child psychiatrist from Harvard, told the Commission that Negro children "become confused and, at a very early age, filled with despair and depression" at the discrepancy between the ethic or rhetoric of equality in the North— 'which is proclaimed'—and the actual fact—'what is.' " He explained:

"They doubt what is; they doubt the value of what is and become rather bitter, rather scornful, rather cynical, and I think at times, rather willful and unable to study—or unwilling to study. Many of the children I have talked with in Cleveland, just as the children I have been seeing now for almost two years in Boston, see this world with a precision and a clarity that . . . I have not always seen. They see what jobs they will or will not be able to get. They see the futility of even the training programs that are offered them because they know the jobs that they will be trained to do will not be available to them in unions or business. They see themselves as cornered, and they see the school as, in a sense, a mockery of society rather than a reflection of its best attributes."

A TIME TO LISTEN, p. 9.

Do most whites see this world of racial tension with precision and clarity? Why?

Why do you think they see school as "a mockery of society"?

BLACK MILITANCY . . .

Many witnesses testified about increasing militancy among Negro youth. James Richards told the Commission: "They [the Negro youth] can't sit back and believe everything they've been told that things are going to get better because things aren't getting better. Things are getting worse, and the children that grew up in a poor area in this generation are getting more sophisticated of what is going on around them, [and they] are going to let you know."

Clifton Jeffers explained that Negro youth are ". . . developing attitudes which seem to say: 'If this society is such that I cannot obtain gainful employment, then I am inclined to pursue that course of action which, in my opinion, will contribute to a downfall, a deterioration, a destruction of that society that denies me the opportunities of employment.'

"I think we find that expressed in a number of areas in increasing numbers. We note the formation of varied and numerous black nationalist oriented organizations, and I think that is a reflection, an outgrowth, of the frustration that the young people face today."

A TIME TO LISTEN, p. 85.

Is black militancy good or bad—for the growth of American society, for the development of Negro dignity, for you?

CREATING DISTORTED VIEWS . . .

Not only can repeated recitals of negative factors continue to create
distorted views of the black community. (I'll wager that most
whites and some blacks would be astounded to learn that, contrary to
the popular impression, the vast majority of Harlem's adult
residents do go to work, draw wages, pay taxes, and have never been
involved with the law.) But a lack of sophisticated understanding
of "the problem" and of the black community at large, so often
painfully evident to knowledgeable black viewers, can immeasurably
contribute to the fear, divisiveness and lack of constructive direction so
widely prevalent in our land today.

THE NEW YORK TIMES, July 14, 1968.

*Would most whites be surprised to learn what is stated about the
majority of Harlem's adults?*

*How would you remedy the lack of sophisticated understanding
of "the problem"?*

LIES, THAT'S ALL IT IS . . .

Inside one of the thousands of Shaw's 85-year-old row houses, Mrs. Washington, mother of four, led me across a linoleum floor to an ancient sofa. Her wiry hair was close-cropped and unstraightened, in the Afro style that currently symbolizes black pride. She yanked off a dangling green plastic earring impatiently and shifted her plump body. She spoke cynically: "Like everyone else around here, I feel cheated. Bad schools, awful housing and it's not safe to walk the streets. White people get what they want. Why don't we?" The bitterness became a mother's sadness. "My son Val gets in trouble with the police just by living in this neighborhood."

I asked her about the government-assisted rejuvenation program that is being planned as an all out attack on Shaw's poverty and slums. In this undertaking, bricks-and-mortar improvements are to be supplemented with programs to improve the economic and educational opportunities for people in Shaw, as well as the public services. "Lies, that's all it is. What they want to do is put Negroes out of Shaw and into some other part of town. They say they're going to have citizen participation in rebuilding this place for the people. I say, when? When's the participation gonna come?" Although Evie has been to citizens' meetings called to help plan Shaw's renewal, she doesn't think they amount to much. "When they gonna rebuild?"

Dorothy Gilliam, McCALL'S, July 1968.

Why does Mrs. Washington feel the way she does?

Why does a George Wallace supporter feel the way he does?

"White people get what they want. Why don't we?"

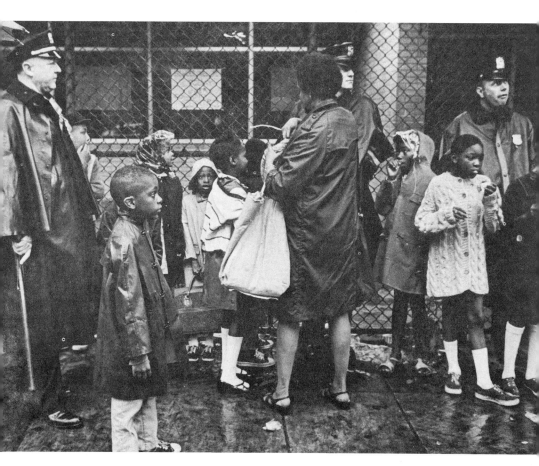

Do you go to a school like this?

How does the cop feel? The little girls? The boy? The mother?

Play out the dialogue between the cop and the mother that is about to take place.

BLACK POWER . . .

Q. You don't think the white man has anything to fear from Black Power?

A. On the contrary. The white man has everything to gain from Black Power, because only as there are equitable relationships of power in any kind of situation can you have either morality or maturity . . .

Q. Does Black Power reject violence?

A. Yes, it does reject violence. It rejects chiefly the violence that has been perpetrated by white people against black people, which is the major form of violence. Even where black people have said to others to arm themselves, what they have said is that we are not going to have violence, and one way to keep away violence is through the threat of counter violence.

Q. What can be said to the white man at a time when he is making more and more contact with black people? What does he have to realize?

A. He has to realize that people cannot be treated like things. When white people say to black people they are going to do something for them, that their corporation, church or organization has decided to do such-and-such for black people, it comes through as an insult—even though people will accept what you are offering them. It does not keep down the spirit of rebellion.

Dr. Nathan Wright, interviewed in U.S. CATHOLIC, July 1968.

Do you agree with Dr. Wright's answers?

What feelings does this girl communicate?

BLACKTOWN, U.S.A. . . .

Blacktown, to be sure, wants more of everything this nation offers;
more education, health care, decent housing, economic opportunity,
and mobility. These can be supplied by whitetown, though not on
the terms conceived by whitetown's leaders. But what blacktown *most*
wants whitetown cannot confer. Blacktown wants independence and
the authority to run its own affairs. It wants to recover its manhood,
its self-love, and to develop its ability to conduct a self-reliant
community. In the best of times it no longer wants whitetown's
patronizing customs and benign guidance; nor in the worst of times will
it suffer whitetown's neglect and humiliations. It wants the experience of
self-reliance, that highest of whitetown's virtues, with all its satisfactions
and pains. Blacktown does not want to withdraw from the American
way but to enter it for the first time. It does not care to be victimized
by whitetown's magnanimity any more than by its machine guns. It
wants to develop its own culture—a "culture that is more moral in terms
of human relationships than that of the rest of society," in the words
of Oscar Brown Jr. In short, blacktown is expressing aspirations for its
own community.

W. H. Ferry, SATURDAY REVIEW, June 15, 1968.

BLACK POWER: HOPE . . .

And suddenly the question of identity has become impellingly important. Since white America seems unready to assimilate the blacks, the new black-conscious leaders respond by rejecting white America. Even the term "black" has become a badge of honor instead of the fighting word it always was, in a society whose everyday vocabulary includes "blackmail," "blacklist," and "Black day." The rise of new black nations was a revelation for Negroes weaned, like whites, of "Little black Sambos" and cartoons of natives stewing white missionaries in iron pots. "Suddenly it wasn't all Tarzan and Jane flying through the trees the way we thought Africa was," says John Torian, 30, a Washington poverty worker. "Suddenly we found these people were talking about independence." The Negro was searching for a past he could be proud of; the new Africa had handed him one and a future to boot. And integration, at least for now, is out . . .

Psychologist Clark for one calls the black power movement a "shoddy moral product disguised in the gaudy package of racial militance," and he thinks it represents partly a genuine Negro fear of moving outside the "pathetically protective" walls of segregation.

But thinking black is by no means the monopoly of fantasts or fools. "The search for identity is growing up," says movement intellectual Bayard Rustin who passed through his own black period years ago. "It will be partly painful and partly foolish. But the moment the society restores the Negro's faith and hope that something will change, the sense of self-pride will fall into place. Most of the kookiness is a reaction to not being accepted: 'You don't want me. OK, well let me tell you, I don't want you, your hair, your food, or nothin' to do with you.' "

"Black Power" may mean guns to Rap Brown, guerrilla war to Stokely Carmichael or bricks and firebombs to the do-rag Nationalists— the angry street corner kids with their processed hair done up in black rags. But to a new breed of Negro politician it is simply a statement of the truth of the matter. White America, they argue, is not ready to break up the ghettos—and the ghettos accordingly will, at some not too distant future day, run the politics of the cities. "We can have an impact in the cities out of proportion to our numbers."

And whites in good measure hold the key to whether the new black mood will prove in the end to have been a painful period of transition into the mainstream—or a signal of the final destruction of the American dream. There is a special poignance in the current state of the elders of the movement. But a society that says it will not reward rioters has not rewarded the "responsible" leadership either. The nihilists who so easily command the television time dismiss the Kings, the Youngs and the Wilkinses as Uncle Toms; the charge is tragically wrong, but the old leaders cannot prove it unless they deliver. Now, even in the time of thinking black, there is opportunity—if whites seize it. The will to self-help has never been stronger. Only the irrationalists imagine that progress can be achieved without white help. But help is unlikely to work, in the new climate, unless Negroes feel they have a measure of control.

NEWSWEEK, Nov. 20, 1967.

In the past black was made a symbol of evil, and white a symbol of goodness and purity. What effect does this have on black people, on white people?

"Integration . . . is out." What is your reaction to this? Why do you react the way you do?

What does black power mean—politically, socially, economically, religiously? What feeling and meaning does black power generate for you?

RACIST-CONDITIONED SOCIETY . . .

One of the clearest points in the report earlier this year of the National Advisory Commission on Civil Disorders is that we live in a racist society. Racism affects everything in our society. Anti-black racism affects black people as well as white people; it is simply the way we have been brought up in a society where one of its values is the lessening of anything that is black. Black people come to grips with it far more quickly than white people, but all of us who are Americans have anti-black racism as a part of our value structure. As I talk about this with teachers throughout the country, a marvelous thing happens. Teachers feel liberated after confronting racism as a cultural value and are open and prepared to take far more positive attitudes toward what they are doing. In the past, thay have been accused of racial prejudice, racial discrimination as an act of the will. This is not an act of the will, and anyone in our society who does not realize that he is racist-conditioned is in serious trouble.

Nathan Wright, U.S. CATHOLIC, July 1968.

How does anti-black racism affect black people as well as white?

Give examples of how a person is "racist-conditioned" by growing up and living in our society.

BLACK AGONY, AMERICA'S OPPORTUNITY . . .

. . . the Negro problem is not only America's greatest failure but also America's incomparably great opportunity for the future. If America should follow its own deepest convictions, its well-being at home would be increased directly. At the same time America's prestige and power abroad would rise immensely. The century-old dream of American patriots, that America should give to the entire world its own freedoms and its own faith, would come true. America can demonstrate that justice, equality, and cooperation are possible between white and colored people . . . America is free to choose whether the Negro shall remain her liability or become her opportunity.

Gunnar Myrdal, AN AMERICAN DILEMMA.

White people cannot, in the generality, be taken as models of how to live. Rather, the white man is himself in sore need of new standards, which will release him from his confusion and place him once again in fruitful communion with the depths of his own being.

James Baldwin, THE FIRE NEXT TIME, p. 110.

WHAT LIES AHEAD FOR THE BLACK CHILD . . .

In 1964, 16% of Negro males aged 20–24 had one or more years of
college—the same percentage as among white males age 55–64
most of whom received their college education 35–40 years ago . . .

The Negro male child is born into a world in which his chances of
reaching age 20 are about the same as a white girl's reaching age 37.
A Negro girl at birth has the same chance of reaching age 20 as
a white girl has of reaching 42 . . .

Today the Negro faces an unemployment situation unknown to the white
for almost two and a half decades. What is recession for the white
—say an unemployment rate of 6%—is prosperity for the Negro. He
last saw an unemployment rate of below 7.5% in 1953 . . .

W. H. Ferry, THE CENTER MAGAZINE, March 1968.

St. James said:
"If a brother, or a sister,
lacks clothes, or food,
and one of you says:
'Go in peace,'
but gives nothing,
that is no use at all."
Today, in many lands,
countless men and women
are starving.
Countless children
suffer from malnutrition.
Many die young.
Many fail to grow, as they should,
in body and in mind.
Whole regions are condemned
to hopelessness.

*Pope Paul VI, POPULORUM PROGRESSO, trans. by R. V. Bogan in U.S.
CATHOLIC, Aug. 1968.*

WHO IS TO BLAME FOR GHETTO VIOLENCE?

. . . There are two theses I believe we can all accept. The first is that the Negro family can be reconstructed only when the Negro male is permitted to be the economic and psychological head of the family. The second, that racism is a blasphemy against the fundamental oneness and unity that the world and all its people derive from their Creator; that racists are, in a very practical sense of the word, blasphemers who set themselves up as gods over their fellow men and worship not a human nature created in the divine image, but the accidents of skin color, of nation, of ethnic background.

In these man-made jungles, there are many who cannot comprehend the very meaning of a phrase like "law and order," for it does not correspond to anything that has ever happened in their lives.

The real issue is: Who is to blame? Is it the Negro man or woman who was born into a miserable, vermin infested apartment, sent to an overcrowded, inadequate school, not taught to read, write or count, and actually educated for all practical purposes in the street? Is this the autonomous, morally choosing individual whom we shall not excuse for his free choice of violence?

The disorder, the alienation, the violence of the ghetto are, to a considerable degree, social consequences that are imposed upon people. It is thus a waste of time to give beautiful sermons filled with words that may make some sense in suburbia, but that the daily reality of slum life has rendered meaningless.

. . . So for millions of people living in ghettos, a discussion of law and order is misleading. For where there is justice and just law, order can exist; where there is injustice and an unjust administration of law, disorder in inevitable.

Bayard Rustin, WHICH WAY? pp. 3–5.

IMPRACTICAL AND IMMORAL . . .

Violence as a way of achieving racial justice is both impractical and immoral. It is impractical because it is a descending spiral ending in destruction for all. The old law of an eye for an eye leaves everybody blind. It is immoral because it seeks to humiliate the opponent rather than win his understanding; it seeks to annihilate rather than to convert. Violence is immoral because it thrives on hatred rather than on love. It destroys community and makes brotherhood impossible. It leaves society in monologue instead of dialogue. Violence ends by defeating itself. It creates bitterness in the survivors and brutality in the destroyers. A voice echoes through time saying to every potential Peter, "Put up your sword." History is cluttered with the wreckage of nations that failed to follow this command.

If the American Negro and other victims of oppression succumb to the temptation of using violence in the struggle for freedom, future generations will be the recipients of a desolate night of bitterness and our chief legacy to them will be an endless reign of meaningless chaos. Violence is not the way.

Martin Luther King, Jr., STRIDE TOWARD FREEDOM, p. 213.

THE SLUM IS ME . . .

You ain't going to like what I got to say, but that doesn't bother me. The only reason I'm here is because the Reverend asked me and I owe him some favors. As for me, I'm fed up to here with white-black talk. The more we talk, the poorer we get, the richer you get, and the better you feel. Well, I ain't here to make you feel better.

I'm 17—my name is Floyd—I got 12 brothers and sisters—and a jail record. I got it when I first started as block leader for my gang two years ago. A landlord waited until a mother of 10 kids was in the hospital, and he dumped her furniture and kids out in the snow. We picked them up and hauled them up the eight floors to her flat. Our gang stayed there with the kids and dared the guy to dump them again. He didn't, but he called the cops and told them I'd threatened him, so I was charged with "intent to do bodily harm."

I didn't have no lawyer and I didn't give a damn besides, so I was convicted and got a suspended jail sentence and a police record. Ever since, the police pick me up any time they feel like it and give me a going over—" cause you got a jail record, hood," they say.

I used to go to school, but I don't bother with that crap anymore. Last year the Rangers controlled the turf where our high school was and didn't let us in for school. They kept about 900 of us out of school for a year, but the school people didn't care because it wasn't so much trouble for them if we weren't there. The cops said it was just two bunches of niggers fighting it out, so they didn't do nothing. My mother said we were going to school, and she walked with us one day and almost got killed herself, so she let us stay out after that. Rather have dumb kids than dead ones, she said.

My old lady, she's okay, but she doesn't know what it's like—I mean, she still thinks that if you're real good and study hard and be nice to The Man, that he'll notice you ain't got nothing someday and give you a nickel. Me? I got different thoughts. I figure that if The Man was so all-Jesus good, he wouldn't turn off our heat in the winter and pay off the cops to forget we reported it or dump us when we get behind in the rent a week. I figure The Man has had lots of time to be nice, and we ain't seen much of it.

We live in a four-room flat, a real dump on the 10th floor, and pay $115 a month. My mother gets welfare and works cleaning when she can and ain't pregnant. Last year we couldn't pay for a couple of months, and the landlord says get moving so my aunt and her seven kids moved in to help pay the rent. Now we got so many kids running around—hell, I don't even know who lives there. Two of my brothers are gone most the time—to the streets or jail—so it leaves about 20 of us in the flat.

Yeah, I want a job, but a real job, not one of them poverty things where you don't do nothing. No one's paying me $1.25 an hour to cool me off in the summer so I forget what a slum I am and smile at Whitey and say thanks. Yeah, that's what I am—a slum. You talk about moving the slum and clearing the slum and building new buildings to get rid of the slum—well, the slum ain't buildings. The slum is me and people like me that you ain't going to let out no matter how smart or nice or educated we get. Man, you've named us the slum so don't crap if we act like the slum.

I got me a friend who took one of them poverty jobs, and you know what he did all summer? They gave him a rag and told him to polish the slide and stuff in a schoolyard. They just laughed about it. "Now, as long as you stay in that schoolyard polishing and off the streets, you'll get your buck and a quarter." Funny thing was, he didn't get paid until it was snowing, and by then he was ready to riot for his money.

Do I think riots is any good? Well, let me tell you, they don't hurt any. Only thing is that the next riot ain't going to be in our neighborhood. If we burn, we burn Whitey, not ourselves. We'll start with Marshall Field's. Why Marshall Field's? Because it's white, man, all white. They don't want us in there except to sweep their floors and haul their garbage.

(*At this point there was some audience dissent and a professional woman who was a Negro defended Floyd's attitude in these words: "There are many shops of Marshall Field stature in Chicago who ask to see my money first if I want to look at a $40 dress. And if I want to try the dress on, they ask a white clerk to model it for me—a clerk in my size—rather than let me try it on."*)

Sure, there are some things I'd like to do. I'd like to fly planes or even fix planes, but that's far out. I can't even get into service with my jail record, and that's the only way someone like me is going to learn to fly. I got a friend whose brother got back from Vietnam, and he don't sit still for nobody. He says he learned to shoot over there, and ain't anybody going to make him Ralph-Bunche-it here. Ralph-Bunche-it? Well, that's like when somebody keeps saying, "Look, you can do it if Ralph Bunche did it." My friend's brother says that when he wants to move to the South Side, ain't no bunch of Polacks going to stop him.

Sure, I carry a gun—got to. The Rangers would take over our block if we didn't protect it. They'd even knife our mothers. The cops don't care. They only care when Whitey gets mixed up in it. My brother got rolled and cut up one night and my mother called the cops four times. They never did come. I got my gun for three bucks from an older guy but I know where you can get one now for two. Night before the riot, some Jews were selling them right out on the corner for two bucks.

Would more poverty laws help us? We don't want any more laws. We're sick of hearing about laws. Laws ain't for us. Our Uncle Toms bought the War on Poverty, didn't they? Are we any better off? We get laws and laws and more laws, and things get worse and dirtier and hungrier. The cops get meaner and crookeder, and The Man talks about Ralph Bunche.

Well, The Man is going to get his. Life can't get any worse for us, see? Can the Church help us? Holy Jesus, that's a laugh. All those prayers and Gospel hymns about sitting back and letting Whitey show us how to be Christian—"Blessed are the meek so they will get heaven." I ain't waiting for heaven, and neither are any other black guys any longer. We want a little piece of this life. And there ain't no Church trying to get us any. Father Groppi? I don't know what his angle is. But any time a white man lines up with black men, he wants something from them. I don't know much about him and his gang, but I know one thing. We don't want anything to do with a white man— preacher or anyone else—in our gang.

What's my future? Haw. Who cares? You don't and I don't either. I think the only one who'd rather see me alive than dead is my mother. No one else gives a damn, including me. So, I got nothing to lose if I set the match.

What do you mean, "I must want something out of life"? What I want don't make any difference. I'm black. I'm a slum. I got a police record. I won't get a good job—ever. If I get married, I won't be able to feed my kids. I'll run out on them, so welfare can feed them. Then they won't have a father, either. You guys hold all the strings so you tell me—what's so goddam great about living?

Chicago teenager as recorded by Dolores Curran in AVE MARIA, July 20, 1968.

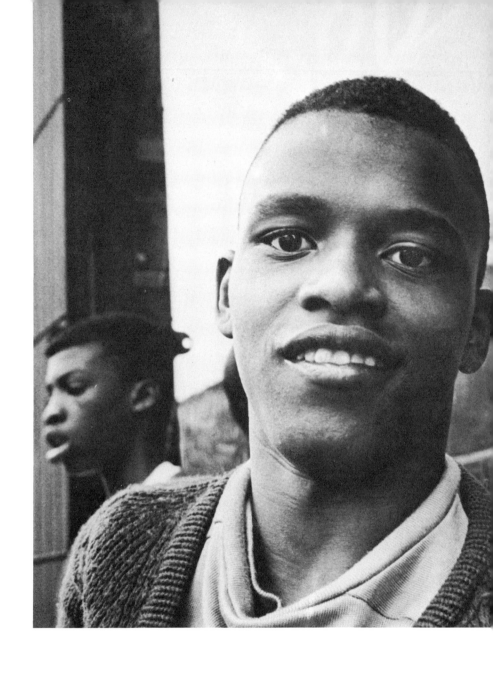

CREATIVE MALADJUSTMENT . . .

This hour of history needs a dedicated circle of transformed non-conformists. Dangerous passions of pride, hatred, and selfishness are enthroned in our lives; truth lies prostrate on the rugged hills of nameless Calvaries. The saving of our world from pending doom will come, not through the complacent adjustment of the conforming majority, but through the creative maladjustment of a nonconforming minority. I confess that I never intend to become adjusted to the evils of segregation and the crippling efforts of discrimination, to the moral degeneracy of religious bigotry and the corroding effects of narrow sectarianism, to economic conditions that deprive men of work and food, and to the insanities of militarism and the self-defeating effects of physical violence.

Martin Luther King, Jr.

Robert Heyer is a Jesuit priest who teaches at Fordham Prep School in New York. He has worked in Harlem and experienced life there for several summers.

Fortune Monte is a young photographer and musician in New York City. His photographs have appeared in a number of national magazines and on educational TV.